AF230770

THE VERY HUNGRY CONTENT CREATOR

By Ellie Gaunt

NOT FOR
CHILDREN'S BOOKS

The Very Hungry Content Creator

First published by Hungry Wolf Press 2024
www.hungrywolf.net

A catalogue record of this book is available from the British Library
Library of Congress Cataloging-in-Publication Data Available
ISBN-13: 978-1-917595-09-4 | Paperback

Once upon a time, in a world pixelated and cursed with lag, a thicc little caterpillar spawned on a forgotten corner of the internet. This squishy dude had one mission: to YEET himself from niche indie darling to absolute clout-chad. But first? Gains. Big, dirty, unholy gains in followers, likes, and content

Monday

Freshly spawned on an obscure blog called QuirkyBanter.net, the caterpillar woke up cringe af, vibing under some leafy OnlyFans content. He posted his first video: a lo-fi ukulele cover of an '80s synth-pop hit. Tagged #altvibes #plzshare, it netted twenty views and one pity like from his mom.

Feeling ratioed, he stress-ate a slice of leftover cake, a cold pizza, and a Taco Bell quesadilla. His guts were already getting ratioed, but the grind doesn't stop. "F in the chat for my digestive system," he muttered.

#altvibes.

Tuesday

He stumbled on a glowing cache of radioactive hot pockets (leftover memes from a gamer server) and posted an ironic take: "Am I the only one who eats these and feels otherworldly?"

His follower count doubled. "No cap," he whispered to himself, his segmented body jittering in MSG ecstasy. "We're gonna make it."

Wednesday

Fueled by new clout, he went unhinged. A selfie under the caption "Just vibing while the haters stay mad" accompanied a mukbang of five cheeseburgers, a stick of butter, and an ice cream tub labeled "experimental flavor."

"Dude, touch grass," commented a concerned moth influencer.

"LMAO, stay jealous," replied the caterpillar, wiping grease off his antennae.

Thursday

Now a minor TikTok celeb, the caterpillar doubled down on chaotic energy. He posted a 30-second montage: a gallon of protein shakes, a 12-pack of donuts, and a time-lapse of his segmented body literally sweating gravy.

Comments rolled in:

"This is cursed but I can't look away."
"New follower, I'm obsessed."

Friday

Somewhere in his tiny core, regret opened like a dark portal, but the caterpillar powered through. He dropped a hot take thread about NFTs and inhaled a tequila bottle labeled "Don't." His insides screamed. "The grindset doesn't stop," he slurred into the void.

Saturday

The caterpillar, vibrating with pure meme energy, posted a live stream called "Watch me YEET my limits." He scarfed charcuterie, mysterious edibles, and waffles drenched in syrup that smelled like burnt dreams. His follower count exploded. Reddit threads speculated: "Is he an artist or a shitpost?!"

Sunday

Overloaded with clout and calories, the caterpillar vibed straight into his chrysalis: a sticky cocoon made of nacho cheese and rebellion. He went dark. Discord lit up. “Is he done? Did the fame get him?”

For two weeks, the internet buzzed with rumors. Then, the chrysalis cracked.

Out emerged not a butterfly but a god-tier influencer. His wings shimmered with holographic filters. His body? A sigma male masterpiece built for clout, flexing abs like a JoJo character. He posted his first transformation pic with the caption: "Y'all built this. Smash that like button, or perish."

And with one powerful flap of his wings, he YEETED himself into the algorithm's Hall of Fame, forever immortalized as a glowing deity of cursed virality.

Ellie Gaunt wrote The Very Hungry Content Creator as a grotesque exploration of the modern artist's insatiable quest for relevance in the digital age. Inspired by Eric Carle's The Very Hungry Caterpillar, Ellie couldn't help but reflect on Carle's early struggle to publish his book, which began as A Week with Willie the Worm. It was only after a Japanese publisher suggested replacing the worm with a caterpillar that Carle's work found its shape and success.

Ellie, unfortunately, found no such editorial salvation. This tale is an unchecked descent into the over-consumption of memes, metrics, and micro-trends, with our voracious creator devouring everything in their path until they become something unrecognizable. It is a cautionary tale of burnout, obsession, and the inevitable transformation into... well, something horrible.

What did I just read?

You have just read a reimagined children's book from Hungry Wolf Press' "Not For Children's" series. As it says on the tin, these stories are NOT for children. In fact they are barely fit for human consumption. They are written by a fictious person called Ellie Gaunt. Ellie is a pen name, they are part of the Hungry Wolf Pack, a collective of weird and wonderfully wacky writers who aim to create stories that make you want to Howl at the moon. We all wear the Three Wolf Moon T-shirt as our uniform, so we are utterly brilliant and ace at everything. But we also use lots of computers and this book was written in collaboration with Kerouac, our resident AI*. Kerouac is trained on open-source materials and a large corpus of our own published and unpublish(able) writing. We believe it is Fair Trained, but it is also trained on the tears of small children, the laughter of bullies in the night, the sound of vomit hitting the tiles at 3am, and some other spinny stuff. So we apologise that what you read can hardly qualify as human writing, but we hope you enjoyed it nonetheless.

*We use multiple custom Large Language Models to produce the writing in these works. One is ChatGPT-4o, featuring a custom GPT trained on a corpus of Hungry Wolf Writers. We also use an offline model running Stability AI's open-source models and Ollama, again trained on the Howls of the Wolf Pack. Most stories are fleshed out from prompts and then put through several LLMs to generate the text, then they are edited by human minds which are just as warped as the machines. For some books we use DALL-E but most are done with Midjourney. Prompts are taken through several draft versions and edits before being sent to our art dept. who tweak out the most obvious AI fails by hand. However, our art team, like all our writers, don't actually exist so not everything we print is perfect, but we try to make products at the quality-level they deserve (meme aesthetic, yeah?). And that's about it. If you read all this and are just fascinated to know more and more and more, then follow the tracks to hungrywolf.net and sign up to get precious intel whenever we hatch another scheme.

About The Very Hungry Content Creator

This work is a parody inspired by themes from classic children's literature but aimed squarely at adult audiences. This book takes its initial cue from Eric Carle's iconic The Very Hungry Caterpillar, a beloved story that itself underwent significant transformation—from its origins as A Week with Willie the Worm to its final, much-loved form. However, while Carle's story celebrates growth and metamorphosis, Ellie Gaunt's version twists these ideas into a surreal critique of the modern creative economy.

This parody is entirely distinct from the original. Its text, structure, and illustrations have been transformed beyond recognition, reinterpreting the tale for an adult audience while reframing its themes through humor, absurdity, and social commentary. We believe this reimagining falls under the fair use doctrine, which protects parody as a form of creative expression.

While The Very Hungry Content Creator draws inspiration from Carle's themes, it does not reproduce his text or illustrations. Instead, it serves as a satirical homage, poking fun at the content-driven frenzy of our times. This work is not a replacement for Carle's original but a playful and unsettling mirror of today's digital culture.

www.ingramcontent.com/pod-product-compliance
Lightning Source LLC
Chambersburg PA
CBHW042158030726
47599CB00004B/784

9781917595094